To Whom It May Concern:

You are the hit
and it releases that
shines through each sky,
every chance you get, deep
down in my heart
you shine on, whenever
any of the little things
that reflect on me are
sometimes never easy, deep

That's a little secret we don't

won't ever go away
even though we don't sha[...]

The Bell That Rang for Nobody

A Study in Moon Blood

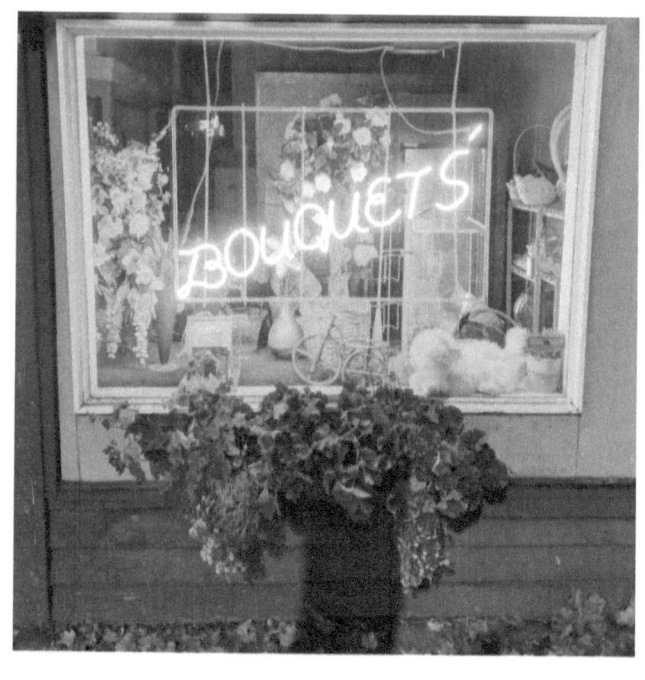

"hooray say the roses, today is blamesday
  — and we are red as blood."
           - Charles Bukowski

blood moon

noun: blood moon; plural noun: blood moons

1. the phenomenon whereby the moon in total eclipse appears reddish in color as it is illuminated by sunlight filtered or refracted through the earth's atmosphere and all its sunrises and sunsets.

"*Your blood and my blood is naught but the sap that feeds the tree of heaven.*"
                                    -*Khalil Gibran, The Prophet*

"*…and the stars in the sky fell to earth,*
            as figs drop from a fig tree when shaken by a strong wind."
                                    - *Book of Revelation 6:13*

Contents

1   tsk tsk

2   Phoenix, AZ

4   Set

5   Only in the Morning

6   7:16 am

8   Skull Flower

9   Smoke Signal No. 2

10   Letter to This Poem:

12   The Bells That Ring for Me

13   To the Girl in the Passing Train:

15   To the Person Who Wouldn't Stop Looking at Themselves in the Window of the Plane:

17   3/13 : Empty Street

18   4/23 : C Line

20   Happy Birthday!

22   To Surrender

23	Mid-June
24	For M.K.
25	P.S. S.P.
27	The Leaves
29	Ratbirds
31	In Needles
33	To A. Karenina:
34	Smoke Signal No. 3
35	Ode to the Flies
37	Captive
38	5/16 : Dream
43	Some Velvet Morning
45	Raster Eyes
47	The Swan Is Dead
50	8/22 : Bus Stop
53	Between Mirrors
54	Rising
55	Morning #10852

56	Don't Wake the Gardeners
59	Au Revoir
61	On the Mountain
62	בדידות
63	Pioneer Square : Molting
64	Drosswalk
65	Smoke Signal No. 4
67	The Bell That Rang for Nobody
68	Morning #10882

XXII

"I entered the cave of amethysts:
left my blood on the violet thorn:
changed my vintage, my skin, and my cunning:
and live plagued by the violet ever since."

> *- Pablo Neruda*
> *Skystones / Las Piedras Del Cielo*

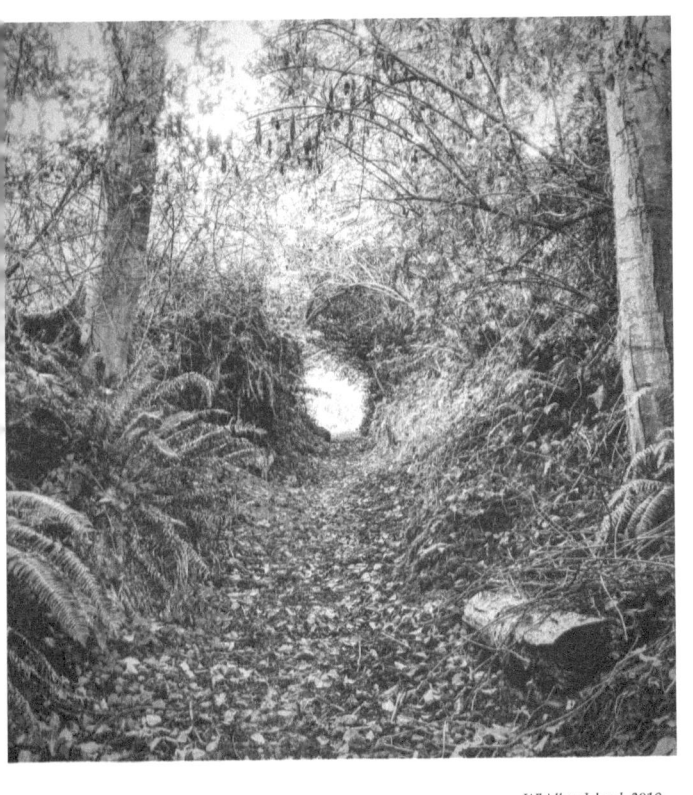

Whidbey Island, 2019

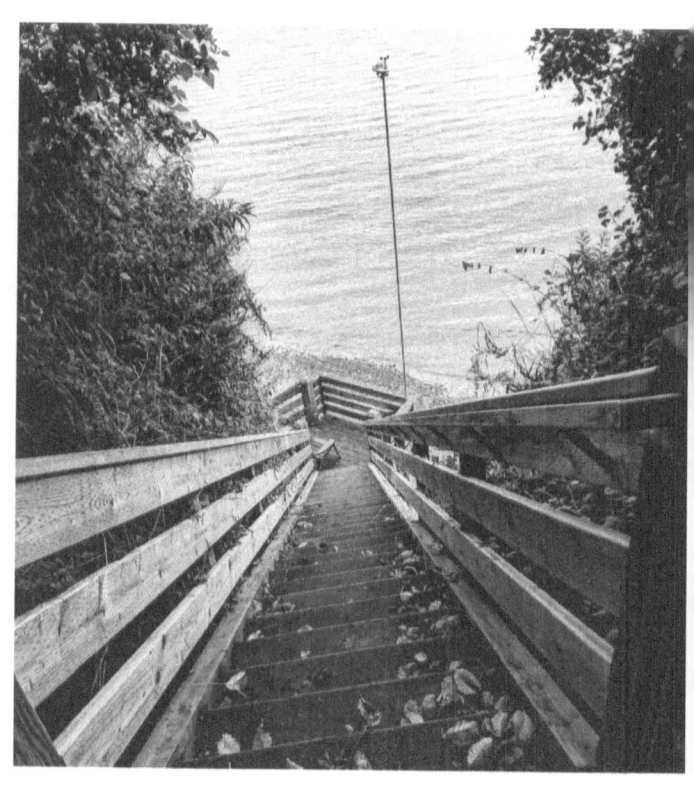

Whidbey Island, 2019

tsk tsk

You are not dead or sleeping.
It's just that some mornings,
beneath the darkness,
you are a blue heron
standing on the sky's reflection;
in a ripple of its own shit.

— And waiting
for any word
to rise toward the sun.

Phoenix, AZ

The grass is dying
on the painted bluff
        outside this window
in this museum of windows.

As distant as it seems,
— with every breath
        the blades fall in.
And despite our canyon,
I can see the ferns curl;
close enough to hear them.

What they are asking
— is whether or not
the place we are growing
is more green
or more beautiful.

I wanted to say no.
Still too green to realize,
that to make us so, — the dead
        fertilize us all.

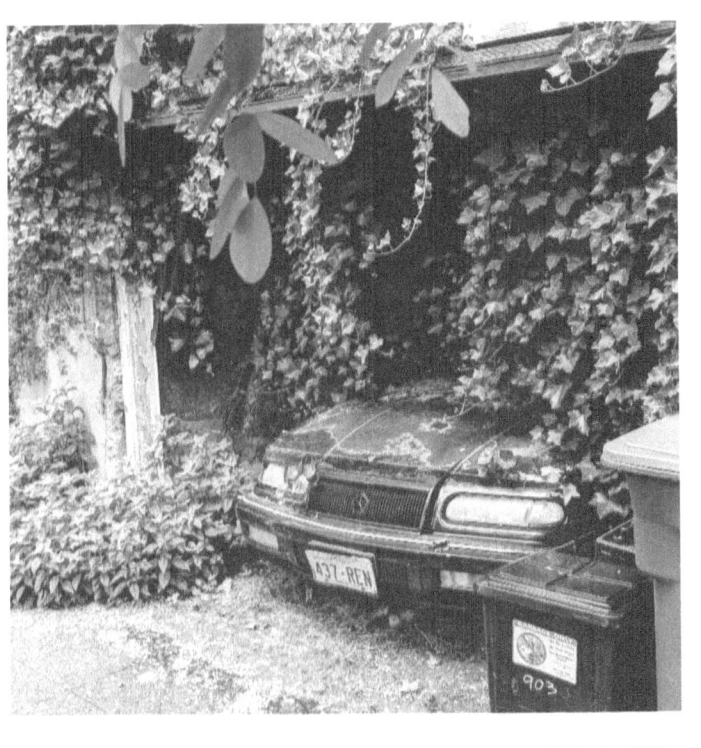

Central District, 2019

Set

No.
The wheels on the bus are tired.
The wind is finding a place to rest,
seeping into the openings:
of cracks in windows
        or the pockets of lost kites
                or yawning mouths.

I can hear — the sewers coughing
as the Earth dresses itself in clouds.
There is nothing to exclaim.
My weather is worn;
the night has idled
and
will not be pushed.

Only in the Morning

Somewhere, last night we
followed the stairs of the subway
— a little too far,
into a giant cavernous garden
that spread out beneath the city.

Filled with old monolithic statues;
        overgrown with brush,
— deflecting the falling water
of some forgotten subterranean river.

And, as we climbed down
past the moon flowers and night phlox,
— that shook from the trains above.
I caught you a firefly
and only in the morning
did it become a dream.

7:16 AM

The drunk at the bus stop
in his singular language and corduroy
in creases, — with his
brown paper teddy bear bagged
up — threaded with a bendy straw,   B-
urps   sips honeysuck, cloudsssunny,
rainbottl, "e *nthazwozsup*"

                 — His pushy eyes,
and the great imposition of words;
stepping all over each other.

       I understood his face;
but the connection was lost
like the two fingers
on his right hand.

— Headed to work now.
But he was right about one thing,
this hide and seek will crucify us all.

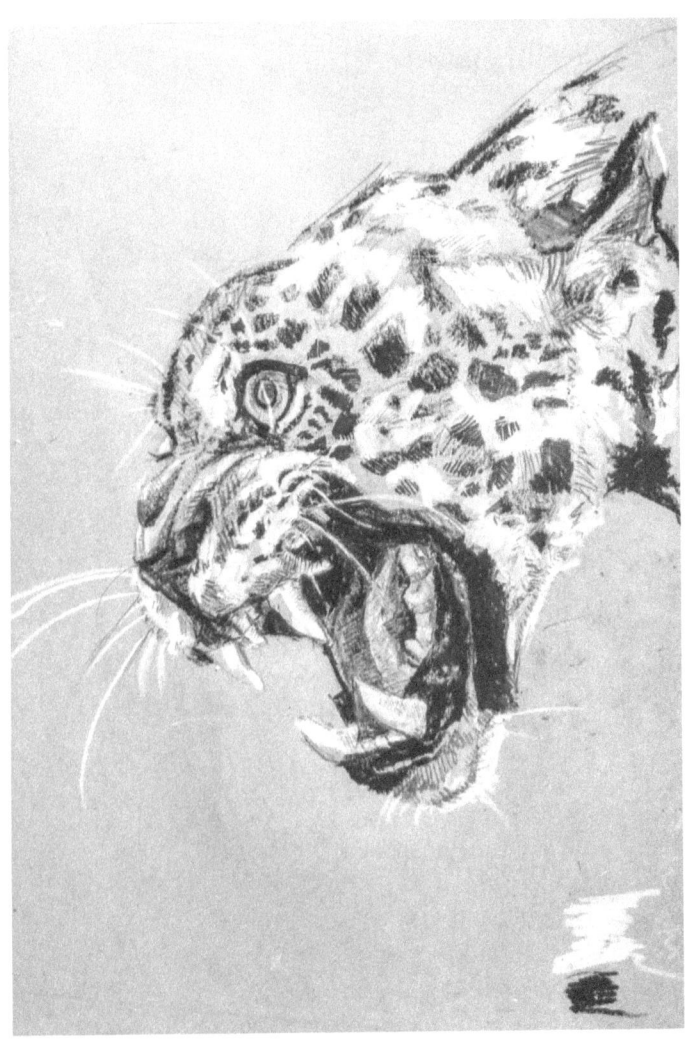

mixed media drawing, 2020

Skull Flower

Trying to collect
the dream I'd forgotten.
The involuntary gift
of decollated flowers
>to imaginary kingdoms
>on grains of sand.

I forgot to capture
the perfect word
>to bridge us
across the river of hours.
— That will come too late
to the receding shoreline,
where I've waited;
>as if there was a choice.
Because I have yet to learn,
to look away from reflection.
So the world is bleached
a blind temperature,
>and colored
by my wasteful motion,
>and swallowed
into the still life of memory;
as the fish who broke the surface
— dissolve beneath the water.

Smoke Signal No. 2

I remember you in echoes.
    Built from too little,
      — now and then your face
        is caught in afterimage
    or ripples of phosphene,
Safe and perfect. —
and I know
when you remove
    your slow kintsugi hands
        from my eyes:
      the ruins will crumble,
    — the petals will fall,
and I will smile;
      Because far away
        — you are laughing
          with your own ghosts,
    but this one is you. —
So we burn songs
into smoke signals
to celebrate what is now
a quiet phantom
— in a sleeping volcano,
    as we wait for our shadows
        to grow into night.

Letter to This Poem:

Listen, you little pansy-ass poem.

You are a thin membrane
      — holding back the void.
I know you must be asking what
your terms of employment here are; but
where is its definition?
Do we live in definitions,
          or in thought,
          or only in its motion?
You seized this world
and made it wait for you; or
pull you to shore.

Were you the first tear;
          or its echo?

We are among the lost here.
You are a frame,
          or a cup,
          or was in it.
You exist for me.
You are using my colors;
          my dust, my ash.
You are not still life.

We are breaking and entering:
to set off alarms, to seed dreams.

The butterflies are drunk
                     — and always leaving.

We are fugitive;
so long gone before
we could ever finish
this sentence

The Bells That Ring for Me

If your words are your own,
you cannot choose what to write.
You cannot choose what to remember
or forget, you are a diamond of mirrors.

Two summers ago:
       climbing the stairs
— passing the window
       of a naked woman, and
          her illuminated contour
                of golden ass.

When you didn't turn around
for another look
out of some false piety toward beauty.
Because you know that its mirage is often
just that,   and sometimes
                the most of it.

To the Woman in the Passing Train:

It was only half of a second we saw each other.
Beneath your scarf, I could tell you were smiling.
Maybe it was just funny.
Me, or that french book I didn't understand.
I imagined myself going your direction:
a projection,
for a passing second.
The shared sunset of a Duchenne smile.

No matter the magnitude,
people are shy with love;
but it's only ecstasy bottled into moments.
Passing just as quickly.
Always fading, in embers.

Born out of its need
in answer to a set of conditions:
— a gravity felt towards things out of reach.
Expanding in a vacuum,
free from context,
framed in a glowing window,
a frame in a zoetrope
of this small fishing town and passersby.

Until we were pulled apart.
Each receding to a point on the horizon,
 _flattened,
into a memory too small to recall.

A flash-frozen portrait
of something lost but familiar.
Dissolved into an idea,
a gas,
into the air.
I breathed you in then out,
like we all do,
— by accident.

To the Person Who Wouldn't Stop Looking at Themselves in the Window of the Plane:

You will never please them all.
Some dogs will always have cages
to bark from.

So — as ugly as you are,
doesn't have to look like any picture.
Nothing has to rhyme.
A song is beautiful because it's true,
yet you feel out of tune
because you've forgotten
that our kingdom is animal,
and its rules are your own.

We all pretend reality
until it becomes itself
       to fall upon;
and we fall together,
in and out of all of it.

I write this,
not that you've asked.
It's just now and then

you are a question,
and you argue yourself into mirrors;
— as if they were mutually exclusive.

Just know,
besides its reflection,
all that is left of you
is forever enough.

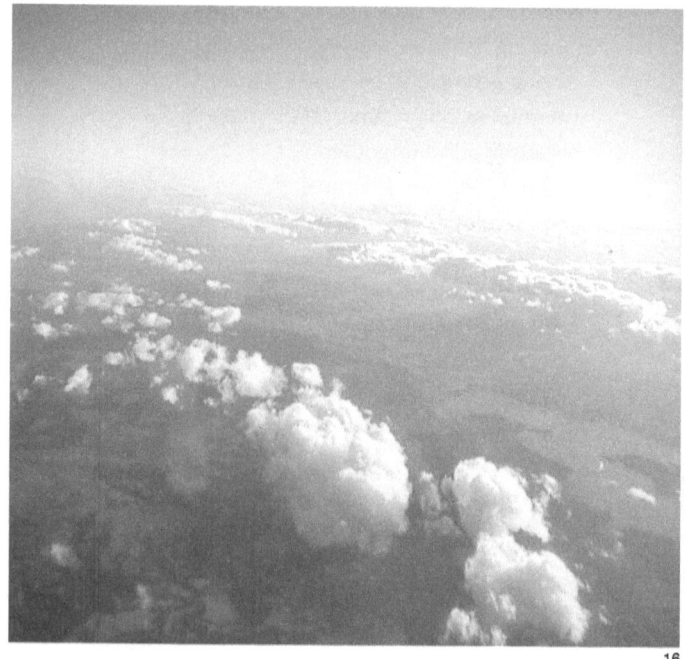

30,000 ft over Kansas

3/13 : Empty Street

I've lost myself in each direction.
I can't be sure of who exactly it is
        that we are weighing.

Against each rock:
hoarding our dreams
hoping one might hide
a clue, or a diamond, or
a bus ticket.

What use is this life spent
wandering through obsidian night;
stars hanging,
        — dripping from the void.
Just to be kicked around
        and tucked away,
while we wait for the world
to speak back at us.
Until we think we are full,
until we are done trying to hear it
and speak again

—what was that? Try again
but louder.

4/23 : C Line

Staring for miles
through the imprinted face
of makeup on this bus window.
A treasure map to nowhere.

— The A/C whines
as the bus caterpillars past a bum outside.
Who grits his teeth in irradiated smile
                and accidental wink.

The days are strobing. My paychecks
                are eating themselves.

There is a grand beauty outside
this tunnel of life,
                seeping, seeping.
— But it's too shy,
and too long
to tickle its ass
for any small change
                or big happy
to happen to   or happen from me.

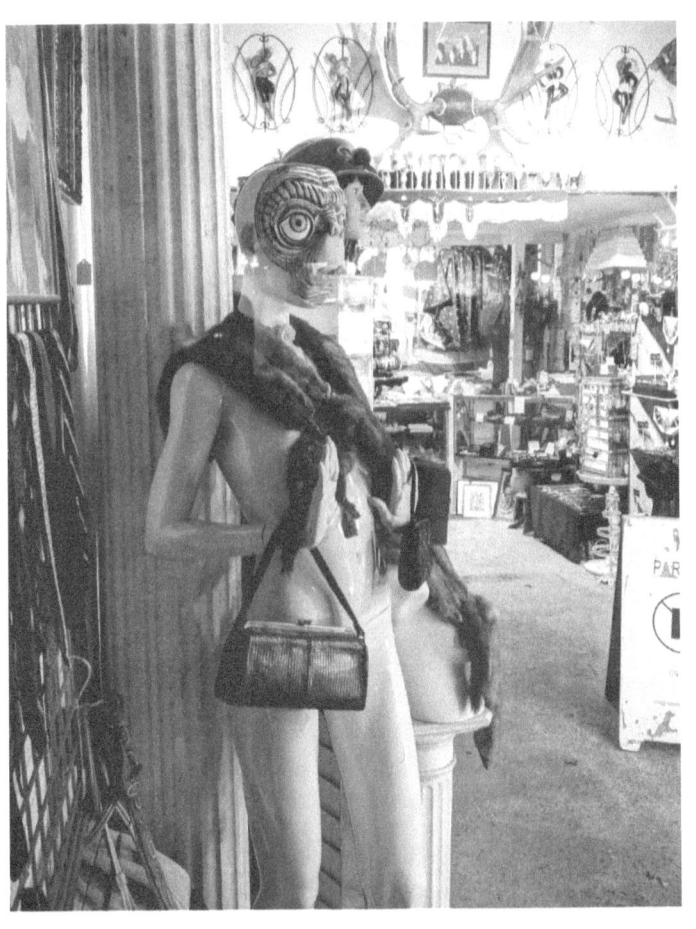

Capitol Hill, 2019

Happy Birthday!

Got laid,
but now this hot swamp of morning
— and bus is clattering.

As we pass the university
camouflage cargo shorts says,
— pulling away his bottle,
"They do autopsies in there
and everyone gets a view…"
…Raising his eyebrows
under his folded brim,
like I give a shit
what's inside:
of it
or him
or me
or the corpse
of this morning.

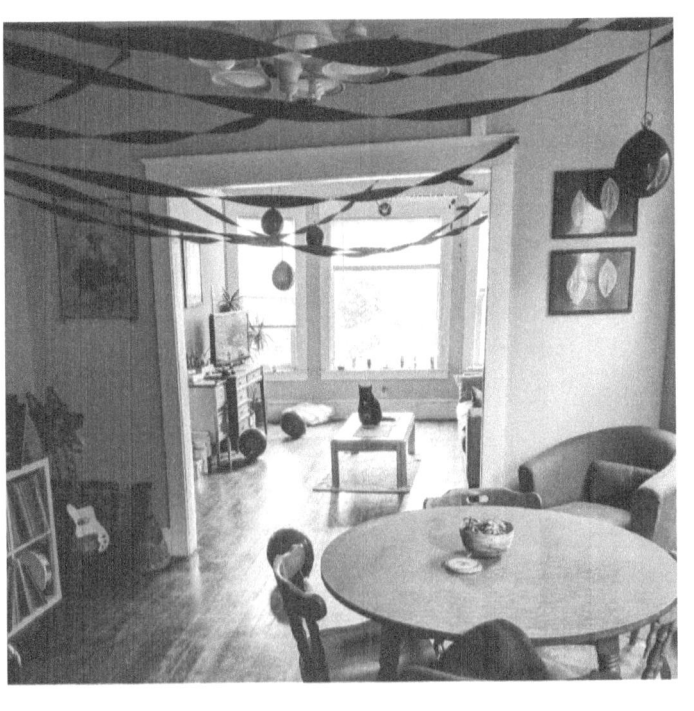

Central District, 2019

To Surrender

Out of sunken beds
— the chosen shoes walk
their morning interrogation:

Under the impatient cosmic rays
past vagrant coin rattle, through
tired beaten doors, for
bad coffee and full rooms
                of empty smiles
                in static exchange.

Until, a small kind word
— wrung itself from clouds in dishwater,
one apologetic ray of beauty:
the warm look,
the gravity of open arms.
A bird finds a minor note
and all the beating hearts receive
alms for the immaculate.

Mid-June

The girl at the vintage clothing shop
steaming dresses in leopard print.

As I turned to leave, you smiled:
— So I ran into the postcard stand
and I am still waiting to be unstuck from it.

I'm not embarrassed at all
but I'm still running into things
and people; — who are not you.

For M.K.

The way the whales sing
into miles of empty water.
— And, how the bird sings
with its own quiet truth.

The way the morning
seems so full of time unspent.

The world expands within you.
Don't let its wealth spoil you:
Savor your spoonful of whatever;
protect the roses,
baptize yourself in fire,
tether your moons.
Write in the dark if you have to.
Love what you cannot.

— And quickly,
the curtains are waiting.
All the grapes will be raisins soon
and the stars are floating away.

Our vastness is not a promise.

P.S. S.P.

All along
the trees have watched
and they know just as little
of what it means
to dress in seasons;
or that our cooperation
        is turning them,
or that our clocks run fast.

To them our dissonance
        ends like a song,
and we share an overture.
So your beginning
is my beginning
— and from it came
a mitosis of the heart.

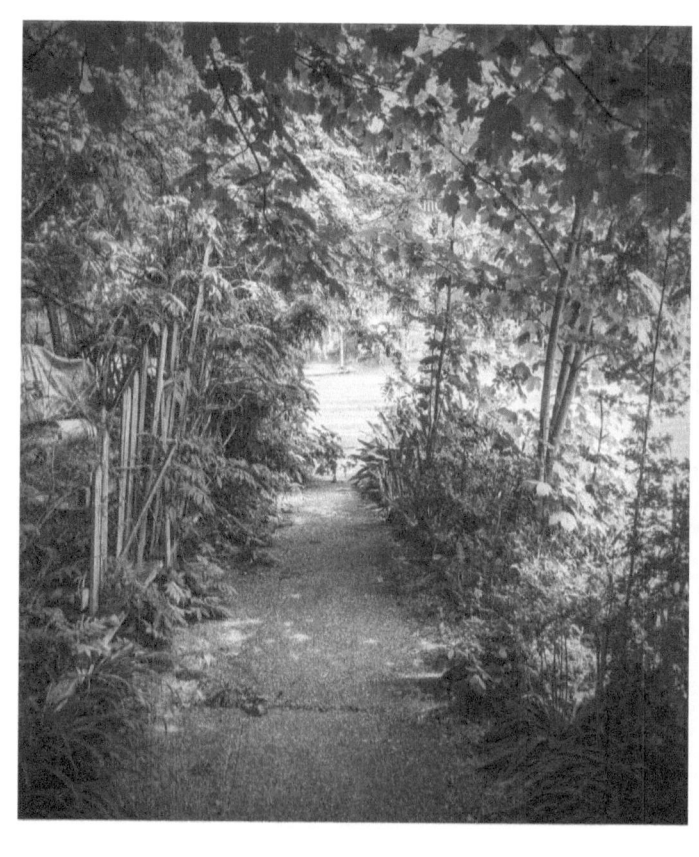

Central District, 2019

The Leaves

Here we are
— sitting or standing
in house boxes or wonder
under the eternal night.

That waits behind
grape skin atmosphere
and its sheer luminescence
in the flat blue envelope of day.

Among the ant-farm
canyons of city street
        or the ancient logic of trees
        in blueprint of life.

We, the leaves — fold it'
s pages back into trees
within this telescopic envelope of skull.
— Because the past, now, is only remembered
and all our stories tell it as it now was.

Until we quickly fossil
and the oil that rises, quiets the wheel
of those who choose to know it as once
                           and twice; me
                           and you.

Ratbirds

Long lives the pigeon,
staring blankly into this.

Their eyes is numberless
clocks — past looking:
past doubt,
past lcd screens, regret, and worry.
In also unchained piety
toward crumb or wafer of refuse
from gone Providence.

Lost and dirty tourists: of alleys,
gutters, bridges, chimneys, churches.
Frozen in breath of the deep water.
All the whys and whos and wheres
— abbreviated.

The real bather of multitudes,
the immensity of the unseen,
and basking within the sum
                 of its mystery.

We cannot taste this.
Not as the: skeleton sheep
        stoned in fear of defamation,
— with our gargoyled politicians.
The angelic feet kissers,
soul drunk saints of ineptitude,
dung beetles rolling crumbs into vanity,
the birds who build cages,
nomadic creatures of fixation.
Holy conditional lovers

waiting for the sense of it all
— in the cradle of our horizons.

…But a dog runs across the park
and my bother scatters with the birds.

In Needles

The bathroom fan is
a swelling jet engine.

When words get swallowed into your head,
and cannonball to your stomach.

When you've fooled yourself
back underneath it all
        and silence is vacuum.

Hallways telescope into great distances,
when searching too far into your own eyes
you find yourself:
        the wrong color,
        lost — without horizon,
a shallow boat
in swirling restless currents
of discomfort and uncertainty.

Until we discover
that all we need is the taste of it
to chisel clay-mash soul
into open hands. To hold
the beautiful nothing
— that is never wanting
but always waiting
for your invitation.

To A. Karenina:

Are we truly an involuntary echo
of what we experience;
and our internalizing mechanism
accords to this witness?

Reflecting — or repeating,
we take turns being each other
in step with fixation,
> on love or loathing
> or only proximity.

This is cooperative
together — or apart,
> and whatever it is,
is held together by all of us
as walking synapses
> holding the web
> netting time into *now*;
> filtering us into *you*,
> and all of it into
> anything at all.

And your end
of this imaginary thread
could never have stopped
> this train.

Smoke Signal No. 3

An ocean so beautiful
that just being
close — is enough.
If there isn't words,
it's because they are too small.

You can stay in your postcards,
radiant and beaming.
Our sand is not each
others. We don't have to touch.
The look in your waves
— was just a look.
But the night remembers you
golden and moon-cut.

The clock drags the bottomless mind
and its ache — in eclipse.
Across the shore, your motion
of here   and gone is
just like
the real thing.

Ode to the Flies

Pity Mr. Housefly — pity,
you have been trapped
and you will never know.
Your quality of life
        depends on doors and windows.
How many times will you hit that mirror,
        or that light?
Before your time is up
            or it kills you.

Poor Miss Fly,
            your eggs are safe.
But how will you spend your day?
Was it long enough for you?
— More often than not
our lives are long enough
but we can't tell christ from a cracker;
        like all you filthy little sexpots.

I just wish
someone would open
the goddamn window.

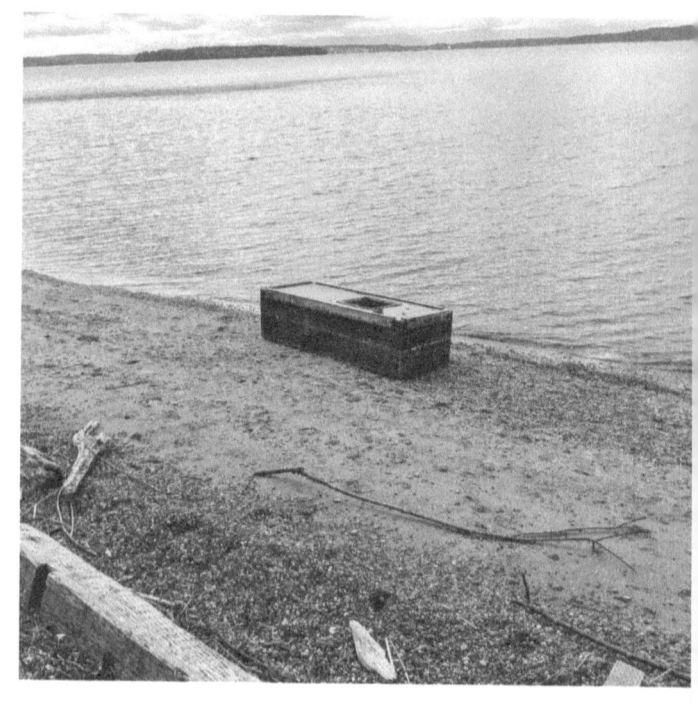

Lincoln Park, 2019

Captive

So if it goes   — that all our joy
reassembles itself,
how do we keep to it?
When does it amount
to something — to save
                or stack
to look upon

                or remember into
                or display in the mausoleum
                of a life well spent?

Like all the heroes — except that
in all their glory and instruction,
they forgot to tell us — how
this very thing, as we hold it,
is worth infinitely more
                than the wake
        of any vessel
captive.

5/16 : Dream

I wake up
to a loud crack in the sky.
Walk to the window,
see the edge of something fly over the house
                and immediately hear it crash
                into the neighbors yard.

I run to the back door and see
in a bush within rainbow fire
a giant golden carnation of a machine
under frozen fireworks, — its petals twisting,
and snap a picture with my phone.
But the glowing lights radiate
and I can't look at it too long.

It begins to rain
                or snow.

— It's ash.
The door closes hard and
I keep peeking out of it.
Soon I notice observational equipment
emerge from its center.

It spies me spying on it.
It could be the government;
                 — no.

Next time I check,
a strangely dressed man appears;
gaunt and loitering,
calibrating the machine.
I take another picture and post it.
The machine's camera fixes itself on my door.
— I run to the bathroom and vomit.
The picture I took goes viral and
I show the visitors I'd invited;
they run for help but return calm.

The machine leaves but always returns.
                My mother comes too
but she does not remember the cat,
and awfully curious about local customs.

— I feel dizzy.
She lunges at me with a red-hot knife.
So I push her out of the window and
her body dissolves on the street.

I reach out to the authorities
but my messages are seemingly hopeless;

intercepted and answered by them.

Soon people around the country are imitating
the emaciated spaceman from my photos.
Friends start stopping by unannounced,
               dressed in his fashion,
always asking about what information
I've given to the internet.
I can't tell who's human.
"Guess who I found outside?" they'd say.

They know I know.
They know I know they do.

I walk to the store, and
everything is not quite the same.
I find cameras everywhere, hidden poorly
but no one sees.

Weeks pass,
the world acts as if this is normal.
The intruders have not left.
— My hair is falling out.
They bring in a taller
more handsome version of myself
and ask if I'd like to switch.

— I cough blood.
They put a handkerchief
 up to my face.
I feel something enter my nose
and prick my brain.
I run outside,

and everything is as it was,
so I go to the backyard
and plant carnations.

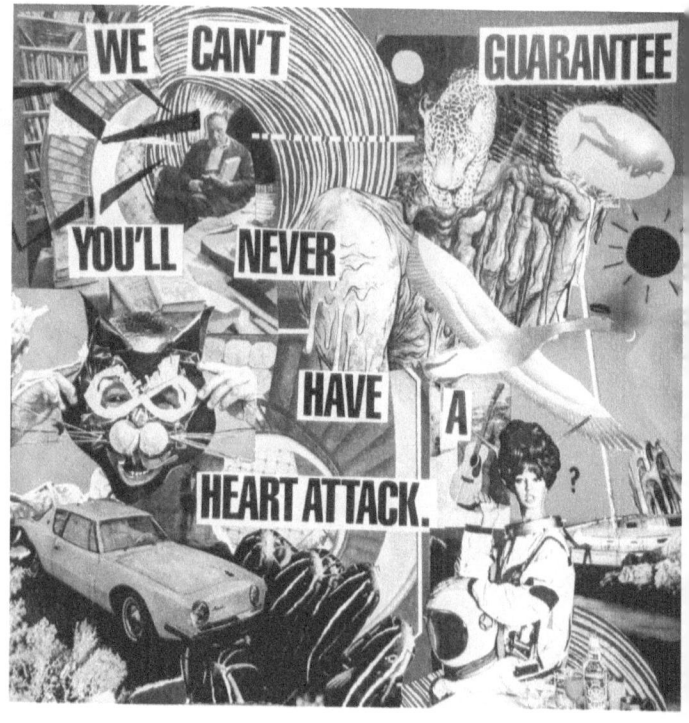

Manifestation Collage, 2019

Some Velvet Morning

To feel
of it all
in waves of fauna
frothing into *this*
growth of wet particles.

— To seed a tree
in five dimensions
and from its slow grain: a
vain flower for God's teeth.

To take your place
in the giant fractal dance
of hello and goodbye
with all hands shaking.

— To sap
the great whole spirit
from void to funnel
into countless tiny souls.

Whose lives happen all at once:
>   in snakes
writhing in global mating ball
and calcify
into fossil-crusted earth.

Only few of which
loop into the ornamented sky,
>   — look back
and see the matter
as verb.

To die and reappear
in hunger or glut,
to love or suffer,
and get born every
morning.

Raster Eyes

Somewhere, — the slow growing sun
wakes behind a clocktower:
        and the city animals yawn
and rise again, in counterbalance
                with the falling moon.
Within the tangle of lives
and streetcar bustle
that swarm and strangle its concrete
                in perpetual motion.

And as you sip your coffee,
a row of footsteps wait for you;
for the Earth's rotation
— to launch you from your seat
                into the shifting labyrinth
                of collective consciousness.
Where there is nothing to do
but move and be moved
in the strobe of days;
— to peep the lens
from cave-painted skull
        and reach beyond its frame.

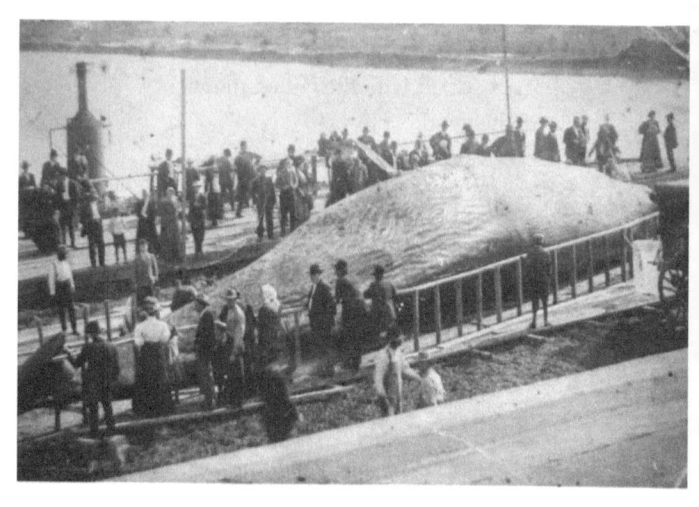

Old Family Postcard

The Swan Is Dead:

its fugitive ghost,
— mirage of love
in vacuum of memory,
a bank of irredeemables.

What vessel could
— hold such a promise;
              or stay
its ever-changing face?
Who could keep
a river
from digging a canyon?
              or even blame it?
And why try to stitch the continents back
together?

With us, born
of its transfiguration
onto the edge of this knife;

a prison of moments

in a cell beneath skin.
Membranes of perception
which combine

                              or divide,
                    or expand,
          or contract
with its secret machinery
of arbitrary physics
from every center of the universe.

There is an aperture to the void
                    even within us
There is an autorefractor.

And if you adjust it just right:
religion is only music,
all books are bibles,
each expression a testament,
and every tongue a prophet.

While God sleeps to become you;
— to speak the music
that holds it together
with every word
a note in rhapsody.

Unwhole
until found holy
               in unbirth

back

        unto everything
and wake again
                as the other side
                of this dream.

Where everything collects,
            every lost thing,

and you look back
over dunes of spent cells
            and find:
the swan is no coiled mortal
and you are the dead one.

8/22 : Bus Stop

Today:
The ember of God's cigarette
was tapped over a Canadian forest,
and so it burns.

Now the sky is full of smoke
and cars wheeze by;
        choke and cough,
        — *smoke and exhaust.*

But   at the bus stop
a grasshopper lands on my shoe
and I look:

beyond shoe,
beneath bus stop,
through the Earth
and all its lava,
and all the water in the Indian Ocean.
Behind the blanket of Heaven,

where all chaos shrinks to order
in the boundless ocean of time
— pinched to instant eternities

by the centripetal life
of mutant dust
on this wet rock
in slow drain to the black hole.

It has all pulled me out from within itself
                    and now I'm waiting
for the sun to thread my soul.

But time is elastic
and spread between false absolutes:

The rain is always here.
       wait
The rain never comes.
   wait
The bus will never come.
— waiting

The grasshopper leaves,
                and all at once
it was as if all the flowers wanted to kiss me.
The day was expansive and beautiful
       and my body walked itself away.

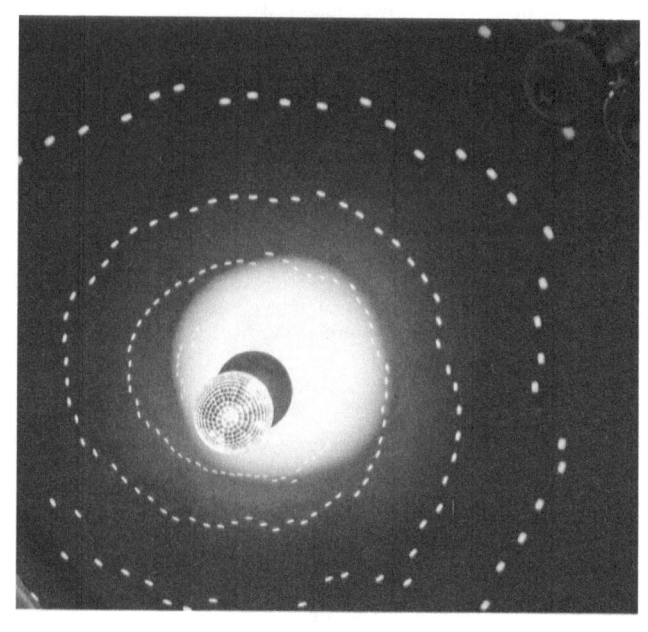

The disco ball in the living room

Between Mirrors

Your lips quietly speak
these words and so
they are written or painted
into your mind.

— And, while your brush moves
to describe my walk
through the leaves
fallen across 23rd Avenue,
the sun above us:
has tucked the shadows
under this row of houses
and the young trees blushing.

As I step on a cloud,
in a puddle, I look up
and face the light; because
you thought I should.
Then close my eyes
to feel the color red
you have chosen
for me, or us,
to remember.

Rising

The water is,
in this small room,
rising under a red ceiling.

The light from the other side
glows behind a corrugated web.
The water is warm but violent.
The room is almost full,
        inches away now.
        — Gasping for air
and smothered by some
figmental Aurora Borealis
and you can't go under
because of course you will drown.

— All you have to do
        is open your eyes
so at last you try
and the day falls in
and pushes you
        out back under
        the totem sun's
        incandescent vibration.

Morning #10852

The roof drips
two stories down
— into a full bucket
on this dewey morning.
There are tracks on the stairs.
The wet paw prints of the silent dog
                mark the steps;
and a broken rope
hanging from a tree
swings slowly
back   and   forth.

All is quiet
but the crows
_ and the low sigh
of a distant plane.

Don't Wake the Gardeners

You, — the flower that bends
toward painted windows:
Did no one tell us there are flies in the honey?
Did no one explain that most of our joy
is from its cost?
                That ugliness and beauty
                    are polarities within us all?
Under naked trees, spring is a folktale.
Until it finds us again in gestures: from eyes
                from hands
                    or winter's grave.

No one looks for rainbows,
they just find them;
and anything is best
from nowhere.
— So thank God
you are too.

As living proof that time is fertile.
So don't wake the gardeners, love
is everywhere and nothing
to wait for.

Still, — we will anyways;
you retrospective angels.
But what is here is perfect enough
for any before or aftermathmatics,
      because we are against it.

It cannot be ruined by ephemerality
any more than our living bodies are.

— And what was here
falls in crystal dust over our cavernous dreams
     peaking our mountains,
     blanketing secret monuments,
     clinging to our oniness.

The Earth will move on, and
more gold will be found in its sand.

We will fill our museums
or find ourselves in those of others;
and sit fat and happy worlds apart.

But I think I will revisit this one.
Where you looked at me
— and we shined for a moment,
                    or evermore.

Au Revoir

Goodbye Chere,
No matter the distance
        you are not lost.
Heaven is within us
and I know you're in there;
drinking wine with Joan of Arc,
discussing battle scars or old postcards.

— And if our bodies are windows
from where you are,

see all the people you've changed
and watch us carve your name
into the tiny corners of this world
as we struggle to fathom its infinite beauty.

Not that it's a competition,

but if there are winners
you are one of them.

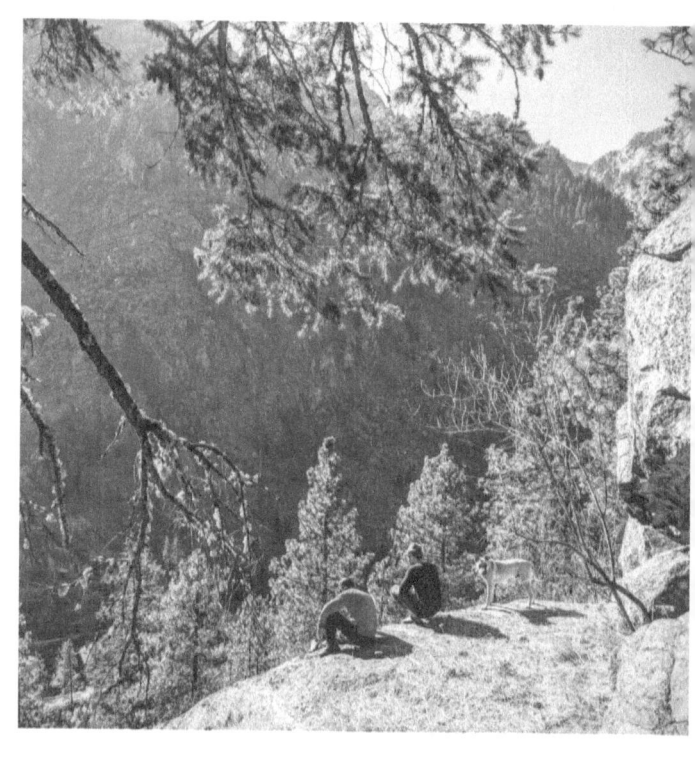

Icicle Creek, 2020

On the Mountain

— This ant is carrying his dead
friend over the cold glittered rock
               we sit upon.
Looking down at the old lonely
house beneath the jagged peaks
that crown this ravine,
               carved by ice.
Still pushing the ancient stream
churning and slowly burrowing
deeper for us to think ourselves into;
               smoothing our edges
and dwarfing us
in the deep reaches of its history
               — to the size of an ant.
As we carry our own lost anything across
this cold
               and glittered rock.

בדידות

The chair across from me
                is empty.
The table is tiled with blue sky.
The dog under the bar
                and my leg
                are asleep.
I don't know
the right way
                to fill this chair
but so far
                its sitters
                don't fit,
and the sky is tiled
                with their names.
Which are probably all
                various translations
of some archaic word
                for loneliness.

Pioneer Square : Molting

Distant star,
orphan sol: as my eyes
reach, I've made you there.
Through witness,
through witnessing your lonely ghost
blink out — morse from shadow.
.- -. .-- .... --- .. ... -.-.- .-.- .-.. -.. -. --. ..—..

What is loneliness
when you're burning?
Chet Baker's love-stoned ghost:
   "To burn too easily,
      too fast."

I walk back to my chair
and an old man in the corner
crawled out of his skin like a cicada.
Now he won't shut up — about his odds with
whores and horses; or about how much he hates
being called a cicada.

The bar candles burn slowly,
and the stars more so.

Drosswalk

Walking
— down the airport sidewalk,
headphones in, but disconnected and hanging:
A crow and a seagull go for the same french fry.
Neither commits, and the rain won't either.

The birds lose interest
— because it was a yellow pacifier,
and even they understood its lack
of purpose; disposability, failure, et cetera.

The asphalt sadly twinkled at the thought,
        under this scummy plastic suck toy.
And it laid there as only a lost thing could.
Described by negative space,
— the void of absence,
the way the ocean would describe a sunken boat
that no one is looking for.

Smoke Signal No. 4

Only just
between you and I:
is a cherry tree in my backyard
the couple blocks to the lake
the lake, and 2857 miles
the whole rolling sky's worth
of indoor/outdoor weather patterns,
the hundreds of thousands
of people who are not you, and all
the good and bad days between
us and the one where
I can see you again.
— Or, in seeing,
just look back
and wonder how it was
that it got behind us.

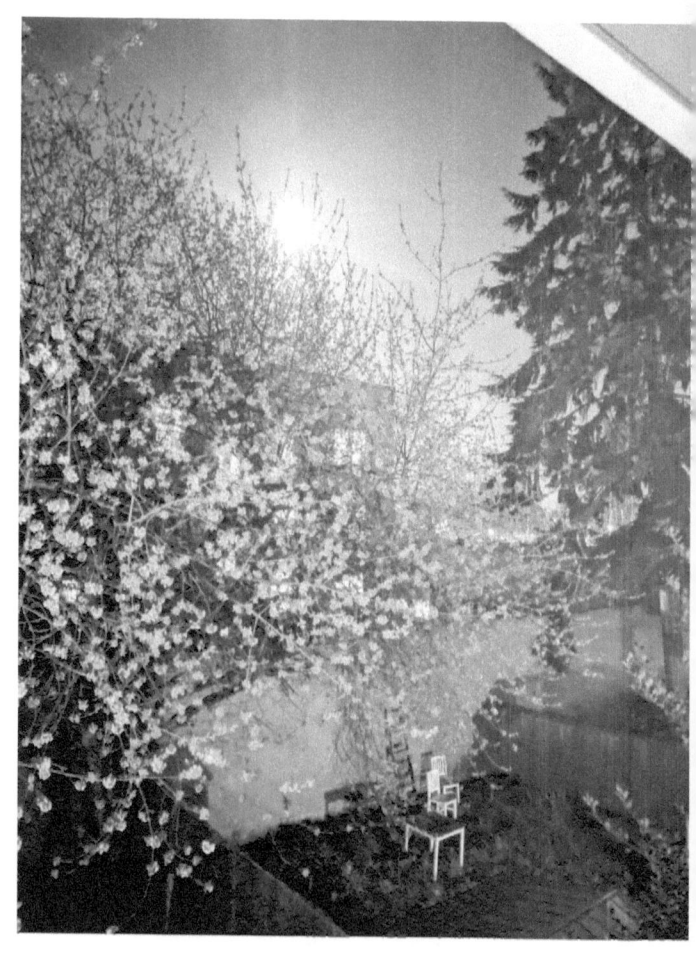

Back porch, 2020

The Bell That Rang for Nobody

After I cut the grass, I saw
a rocket emerge from the sea. I

watched western movies as the sun
set and stood where I am standing,

enveloped in porchlight. A dumb
witness to the pink moon and all the golden
windows of those swept in from darkness.

TV blue waves contouring faces, every direction,
in unimaginable distances. Trees

hush the honk and siren under-
glow of wool blanket over city.

And now after all that
has been, each story

with its ending, I pretend

it's all frozen because beyond it
's motion and the reach of its bells,

not one cricket is chirping.

Morning # 10882

I am writing this
but caught in a conversation happening
in another room.
My thoughts are perforated with rising words.
Morning cars bumble up and down the street.
Wet tires on a world abbreviated to roads,
                        — to headlines.
'Astronomical' Surge Leads to Quarantine Warning
Kenny Rogers, Dead at 81
Fat Cat Sits on Table Staring

I am writing this
from a receding kitchen chair, casting
my disquietude to the future.
Where each sky is unique and falling,
Where all life has already been suspended.
And the fridge rattles and kicks on.
Nearly A Million Children Left Behind In Venezuela
As Parents Migrate
Who Should Be Saved First? Experts Offer Ethical
Guidance

I am writing this, burning
my engine on oatmeal and watery coffee;

jobless and guilty of smoking
                    too many cigarettes about it.

Now the moment is finally quiet
so I begin to collect myself and find nothing.
Someone downstairs flushes and laughs.
Five Adaptable Recipes, All From Your Pantry
a ranking of 'The Best Canned Tomatoes'
As Tourism Plummets in Thailand, Elephants Are
Out of Work, Too.

You are reading this
like a poorly made coloring book
with everything in your periphery calling
to be seen. Waiting to be
collapsed and taken with,
                    of this I am also guilty;
consolidating myself to fit in the caravan
with everything else that was.
By the way, thank you again
                    and where to now?

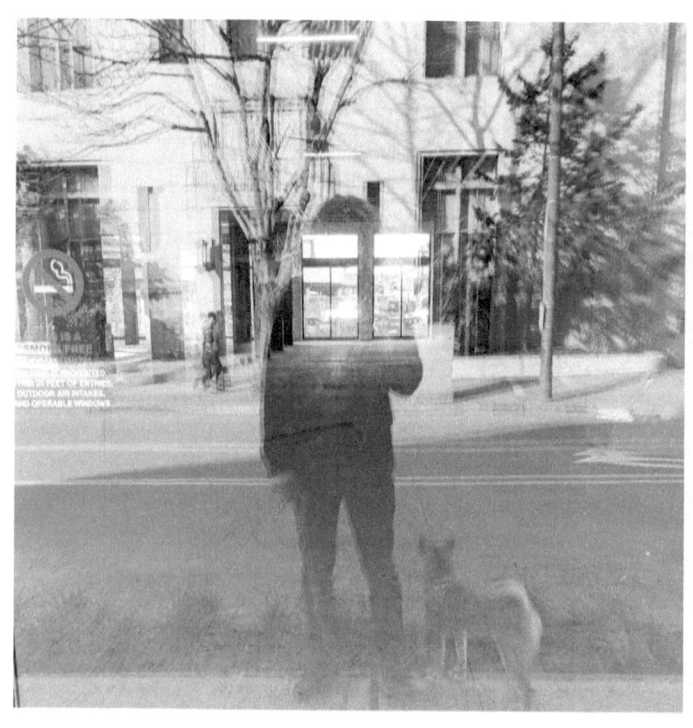

Pioneer Square, 2019

www.ingramcontent.com/pod-product-compliance
Lightning Source LLC
Chambersburg PA
CBHW020604220526
45463CB00006B/2439